THE STORY OF THE EARTH
CAVE

LIONEL BENDER

FRANKLIN WATTS
New York · London · Toronto · Sydney

© 1989 Franklin Watts

First published in the USA by
Franklin Watts Inc.
387 Park Avenue South
New York, N.Y. 10016

Library of Congress Cataloging-in-Publication Data

Bender, Lionel.
    Cave/by Lionel Bender.
    p. cm – (The Story of the Earth)
    Bibliography: p.
    Includes index.
    Summary: A geological explanation of the reasons and
    ways in which caves are formed with a discussion
    of their uses throughout history.
    ISBN 0-531-10819-8
    1. Caves – Juvenile literature. [1 Caves.] I. Title.
    II. Series: Bender, Lionel. Story of the Earth.
GB601.2.B46 1989
551. 4'47 – dc19   89-5531 CIP AC

Printed in Belgium

Consultant Dougal Dixon

Designed by Ben White

Picture research by Jan Croot

Prepared by Lionheart Books
10 Chelmsford Square
London NW10 3AR

Illustrations
Peter Bull Art

Photographs
GeoScience Features *Cover*, 1, 6, 7, 8, 9, 11, 19, 22,
    23, 24, 27,
Survival Anglia 17,
Dr A. C. Waltham 12, 15, 18, 20, 21, 25, 28, 29, 31

THE STORY OF THE EARTH
CAVE

LIONEL BENDER

CONTENTS

This book tells the story of a typical cave. A cave is a hollow beneath the surface of the Earth. Limestone rock is broken down into tiny pieces, or dissolved, by the acid in rainwater. The dissolved rock is washed away by streams that work their way underground, leaving holes and tunnels. The tunnels develop into cave systems.

▽ The illustration shows a section through a limestone landscape, with caves at different stages of development. In the limestone cliff on the left, an underground stream is carving out a cave system. Across the valley is another limestone hill in which an old cave system has finally collapsed, leaving a deep valley, or gorge.

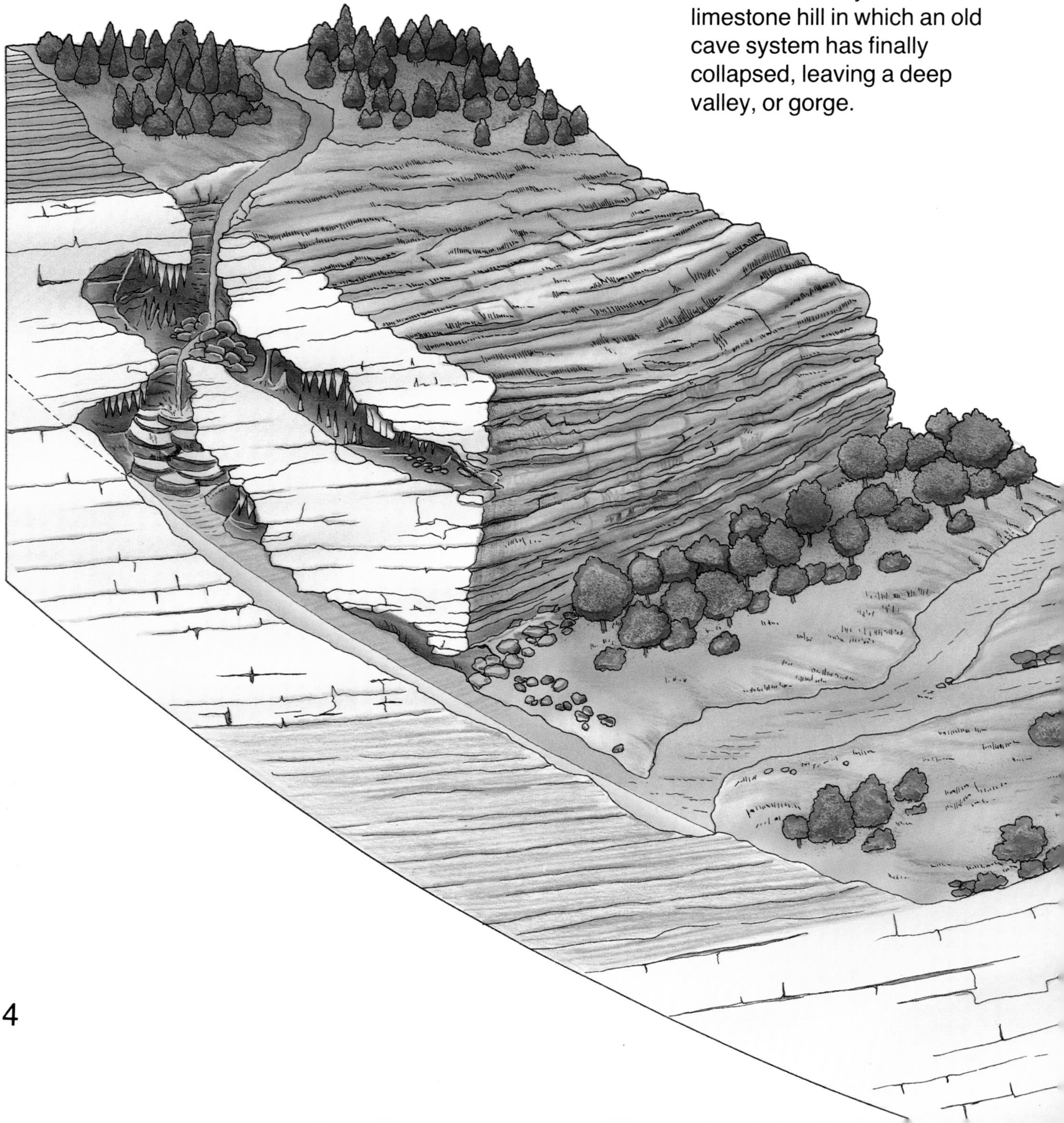

Cave systems form and get larger as the tunnel roofs collapse and underground streams change course. Chemicals in the dissolved limestone collect as solid material and form underground structures of strange shapes. Eventually the caves may become so big that whole systems collapse, leaving the hollows open to the sky.

▽ We have divided the story of our cave into ten stages. In the following pages of the book we look at each stage in turn. There are photographs of caves in different parts of the world. Diagrams show how a cave forms and changes with time. We also look at the wildlife in caves and how caves affect people.

On the surface of land between two hills is a region of limestone. Limestone is a rock made of the mineral calcite. In some places calcite forms chalk. The rock was formed on a seabed millions of years ago, but it is now exposed to the air. Rain that falls on the limestone contains some carbon dioxide gas from the air and has formed a weak acid. This acid "eats into" the limestone and dissolves it slowly but continually.

▷ The acid in rainwater attacks the limestone along any cracks or weak lines in its surface. It widens the cracks and wears them into these wide channels.

▽ Between the channels the limestone is left as rounded masses that look like paving stones. These are sometimes called grikes. The whole landscape is barren, as here in Yorkshire, England.

The stream disappears

A stream that flows down from the hills contains some of the acid from the rainwater. When the stream reaches the limestone area, it flows down into the channels, dissolving and washing away more of the rock.

Over many years, the stream slowly wears away a shaft straight down through the rock. This is called a swallow hole or sink hole, and the stream flows down it and underground. In limestone areas, some streams disappear underground, leaving a dry valley on the surface.

◁ A river tumbles into a rocky shaft and flows downhill underground. The shaft has been worn into the limestone hills by acid in the river water. This shaft, or sink hole, in Yorkshire, England, is known as Jingling Pot.

▷ Only a tiny stream now runs along this wide valley. The valley was carved out millions of years ago by a river that once flowed between the hills. The river formed a sink hole and disappeared into it, flowing underground.

The stream tumbles straight down through the shaft until it reaches an area deep inside the hills where there is no limestone, but a type of rock that acts like a sponge. This rock is full of water – it can hold no more.

The upper level of the water filling the rocks is known as the water table. When the stream reaches the water table it starts to flow flat along the land, forming a small underground river.

▷ An underground stream cannot wear its way further into the limestone than the level of the water table. Instead it wears away, or erodes, the rock either side to form a tunnel, and it flows along this. For much of the time the stream fills the tunnel completely. But in dry seasons there may be no more than a trickle of water along the tunnel floor.

▽ A stream or river flowing underground and across the water table may eventually reappear at the foot of a hill. It then wears away a valley on the surface of the land.

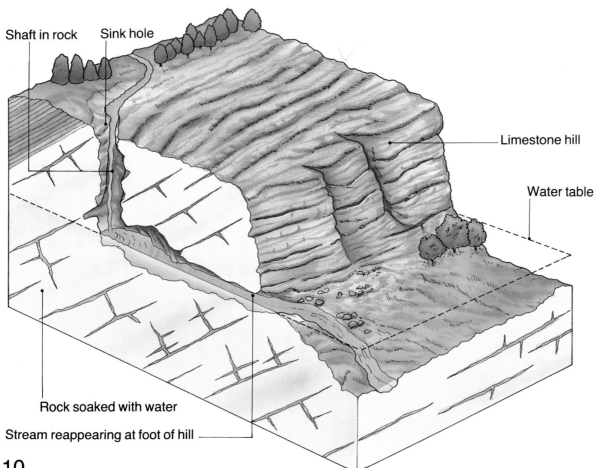

Shaft in rock   Sink hole

Limestone hill

Water table

Rock soaked with water

Stream reappearing at foot of hill

△ A stream flowing underground forms a smooth-sided tunnel in the rock. When the height of the water table changes, the stream flows at a different level and begins to carve out a new course. The old water-course is left as a dry tunnel, or gallery. This gallery is in the cave Ogof Ffynnon Dou in Wales.

Underground, the stream weaves from side to side, just as it did on the surface. It flows round areas of hard rock and wears away tunnels through weaker rock. All this happens along the level of the water table.

Over a period of hundreds of years, the land becomes drier. The water table is now lower than before. The stream no longer flows along its old course, but works its way deeper underground and forms a new tunnel.

▽ In a limestone hill, a whole series of galleries can be carved out by underground streams. Each gallery shows where the different levels of the water table once reached. The stream flows in the lowest tunnel, where the water table is. The stream has made its way to this level through sink holes which link each gallery.

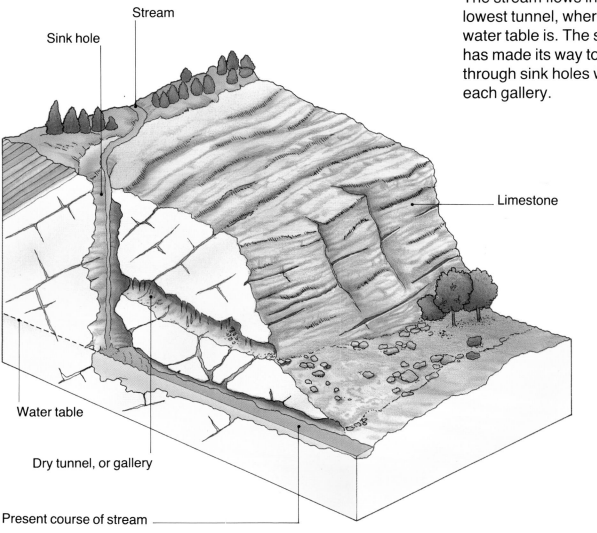

Stream

Sink hole

Limestone

Water table

Dry tunnel, or gallery

Present course of stream

Throughout the limestone region, water is seeping through the land. It widens underground channels and weakens the solid structure of the rock. In a few places the rock above a tunnel or gallery has been made so weak that the ceiling collapsed. This has created underground halls and dome-shaped chambers. These are the caves.

The floors of the caves are strewn with the broken-off chunks of rock. The underground stream has carried away the smaller chunks, but the rest remain as huge mounds of rubble.

▷ The roof of a cave can fall in at any time, blocking galleries and enlarging the underground hollows. Many of the hollows formed in this way are tens of feet high and wide, as here at Piaggia Bella Cave, Italy.

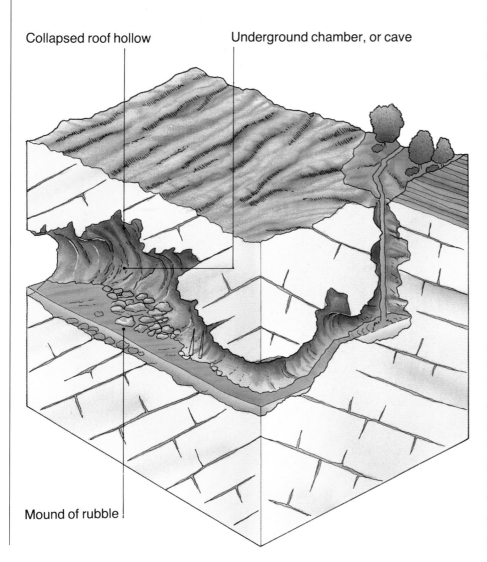

Collapsed roof hollow

Underground chamber, or cave

Mound of rubble

◁ There is a constant trickle of rainwater through the rock from the surface of the land. This slowly dissolves the calcite. Eventually the cracks deep in the rock become so wide that huge blocks of limestone are left hanging above the open spaces. These blocks drop to the floor of the cave under their own weight.

Life in a cave

Caves are usually damp, dark and cold places. Yet several types of animals and plants live in them. Many of the animals spend all their lives in the caves. They feed either on plant remains that are washed from the surface of the land by underground streams, or on each other. A few animals, such as bats, go into caves only to rest or to take shelter from the weather. Most of the plants that grow in caves are mosses, lichens and fungi, which need little or no sunlight.

▷ At the entrance of the cave is the "light zone." Some sunlight reaches here, and in little patches of soil, green plants such as ferns grow. Further into the cave is the "twilight zone." This gets very little light. Here bats and swifts roost, mosses and lichens grow on the rocks, and snails cling to the walls.

In the "dark zone" deep inside the cave, frogs, newts and fish live in the waters, and spiders crawl about on the damp walls.

▷ This long and slender animal with little legs is an olm. It lives in waters deep inside many of the caves of eastern Europe. Living in total darkness, the olm has no need for eyes and so is blind. Its body is white – there is no need for bright skin colors.

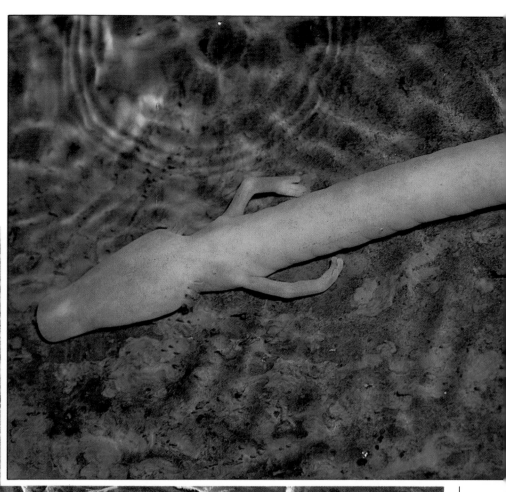

The trickling water dribbles out of the rock on the cave's walls. Some of the carbon dioxide it contains returns to the air. As a result, the water can no longer hold on to the dissolved calcite. The calcite collects on the surface of the rock, layer by layer. In places it forms a smooth covering over the cave wall. Elsewhere in the cave, it builds up into oddly shaped structures.

▷ Over thousands of years, little curtains of calcite may form along the lines of cracks in a cave roof. The calcite also forms long thin cones that hang down from the roof, as here. On side walls, the calcite may build up into masses that look like balconies.

▽ The calcite in an underground river gradually builds up into a series of terraces, or gours, on the river bed. In this cave in France, known as the Gouffre Berger, there are many huge gour pools.

A thin layer of glistening moisture covers the ceiling of the cave. This is where calcite is being deposited. Long, thin, hanging structures known as stalactites are forming. These grow in size like icicles, drop after drop.

There are stalactites of all shapes – straws, needles, curtains and carrots – and, in places, there are thousands of them grouped together. Chemicals washed from the rock by the stream have colored some of the stalactites.

◁ A brightly colored curtain stalactite has formed on the sloping ceiling of this cave, Grotte Père Noël, in Belgium. Rainwater often washes from rocks chemicals containing iron, copper and zinc. Iron turns the stalactite red, copper colors it blue and zinc turns it yellow.

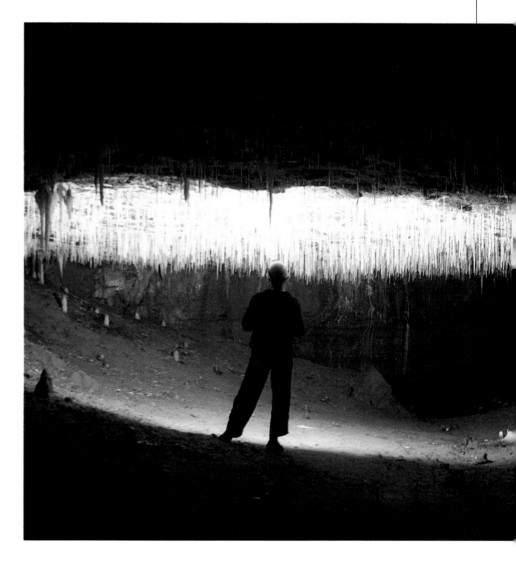

▷ In this dry cave tunnel in Ease Gill Cavern, Cumbria, England, a mass of straw-like stalactites cover the ceiling.

Water dribbles down the sides of the stalactites and drips off the ends. Each drop hits the floor of the cave with a splash. The force of the impact deposits particles of calcite on the floor.

After millions and millions of drips, the particles of calcite have built up on the cave floor into a structure that looks like a stalactite turned upside-down. This pillar of calcite is known as a stalagmite.

▽ Some stalagmites resemble pine cones. Others look like knobbly pillars or stacks of saucers. Stalagmites are usually shorter and thicker in width than stalactites. These lumpy stalagmites are in the Postojna Caves in Yugoslavia.

△ A stalagmite forms on the cave floor directly beneath a stalactite. The two structures grow towards one another very slowly. Eventually they may meet and form a solid column of calcite. This column is in La Gournier Cave in France.

The column becomes thicker and thicker as more layers of calcite are laid down around the outside. Cut across, the column would show growth rings like those seen in a cross-section through a tree trunk.

The underground stream continues to flow through the rock, wearing away tunnels as it goes. Along one tunnel, the mass of rock ends in a cliff. Here the stream gushes out into the daylight once more. From the base of the cliff the stream runs along the surface of the ground once more, as it did between the hills above the cave.

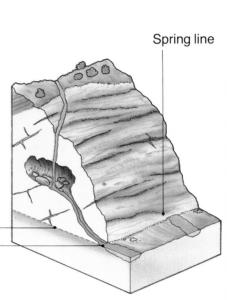

◁ An underground river flows out into daylight from the largest cave entrance in Europe – an exit from the Grotte Bournillon cave system in France.

◁ △ The place where an underground river flows out from a hill or cliff is known as a resurgence. This resurgence is in the Jura Mountains in France. Often, the water table is at the same level as the bottom of a mountain or hill. Where this happens, there may be a line of resurgences and streams along the bottom of the hill. This is called the spring line – a spring is the name for the start of a stream.

25

Only a gorge remains

All the time that the stream has been flowing through the cave, it has been wearing away at the walls and ceilings of the underground tunnels. Chunks of rock have been falling off the cave ceiling, enlarging the chamber upwards.

Suddenly, and without warning, the whole roof of the cave falls in, opening the dark depths to the sky. In time, the roof of each tunnel and gallery collapses, forming a steep-sided gorge.

▷ A river flows along the bottom of a gorge created by a collapsed cave sytem. Beneath the hills in which the cave system formed are layers of rock which stop the water seeping underground.

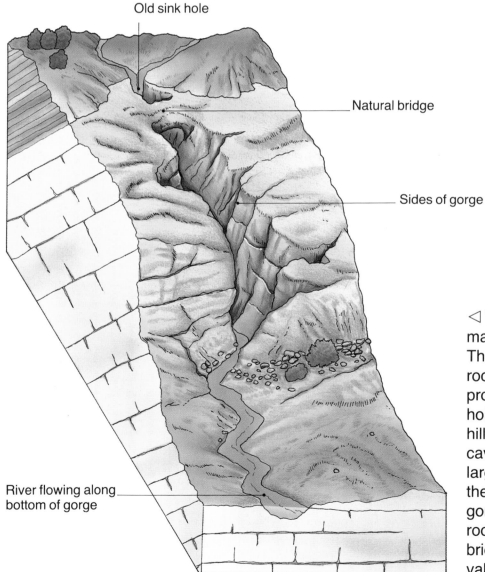

Old sink hole

Natural bridge

Sides of gorge

River flowing along bottom of gorge

◁ The collapse of a cave roof may not happen all at once. The thinnest parts of the roof rock fall in first. This produces a series of deep holes on the surface of the hills, following the line of the cave. The holes become larger and larger until some of them join together to form the gorge. Parts of the old cave roof remain as natural bridges across the new river valley.

Limestone landscapes are bleak and dry. They do not form good soils, so people do not farm on them. The caves beneath the surface, however, can be used by people as shelters. At the end of the last Ice Age, about 10,000 years ago, people in many parts of Europe used caves as their homes. They made woodfires in the cave to keep warm and to provide light, and they kept animals, both for food and as pets.

Nowadays, there are not many cave-dwellers (except in artificial rock hollows), but limestone caves still attract many tourists and sports people.

▽ Here, at Niah Cave in Sarawak, Borneo, local people live and work, as they have done for many generations. The entrance to the cave provides them with a safe, dry place to make their homes. Inside the cave, swifts roost and nest in their thousands. The people collect and sell the birds' nests, which are used to make soup.

△ Cave exploration is a popular sport. The
sport is called spelaeology, sink-holing, or
spelunking. Teams of people go into caves
heavily equipped with flashlights and climbing
gear. They explore the underground tunnels.
galleries and streams.

Acid A hydrogen-containing chemical that reacts with substances containing a metal such as copper, zinc, or iron. In the reaction the hydrogen of the acid is replaced by the metal to form a salt.

Calcite A mineral made of the metal calcium with carbon and oxygen – the chemical name is calcium carbonate. Calcite is the mineral of which many forms of limestone are made, including chalk, fossiliferous limestone, coral rock, and dripstone. The last is the general name for the rock of cave systems with stalactites and stalagmites.

Channel A large crack in limestone rock formed by rainwater seeping into the rock and wearing it away.

Dissolve To break up by the action of water. When a substance dissolves, it breaks down into its tiniest particles and these are mixed with the water and washed away.

Erode To wear away. For example, rainwater erodes limestone rock, making tiny cracks in the rock into large channels and forming hollows that become caves.

Gour A natural dam or terrace of calcite that forms across an underground stream. The calcite is laid down on the bottom of the stream as the water flows over a bump.

Limestone A "soft" rock made up of the mineral calcite. It is formed over millions of years on seabeds. Sometimes it is made up of the calcium carbonate of the shells of sea animals.

Sink hole A tunnel, or shaft, that leads straight down through limestone rock. It is formed by a stream wearing the rock away.

Stalactite A growth of calcite downward from a cave roof.

Stalagmite A growth of calcite upward from a cave floor.

Water table The upper surface of a region of rock that is permanently soaked with water so that it can hold no more.

Deepest cave
Gouffre Jean Bernard, in France, is the deepest cave known. The cave lies 1,535 m (5,036 ft) beneath the surface of the ground.

Longest individual cave
Lubang Nasib Bagus, a cave in Gunung Mulu National Park in Sarawak, Borneo, is the largest cave known. It has dimensions of 700 m (2,300 ft) long by 300 m (980 ft) wide and 70 m (230 ft) high. It is big enough to hold an aircraft carrier and still leave room to fly the airplanes.

Longest stalactite
A stalactite in the Cueva de Nerja near Malaga in Spain is 59 m (195 ft) long – longer than the Statue of Liberty in New York is tall.

Tallest stalagmite
La Grande Stalagmite in the cave of Aven Armand in France is 29 m (98 ft) tall.

Longest continuous column of calcite
The Flying Dragon Pillar is a calcite column 39 m (128 ft) tall. It has formed as a stalactite that joined with a stalagmite above it. The Pillar is in the Nine Dragons Cave in China.

In Ogle Cave, New Mexico, the Bicentennial Column is 32.3 m (106 ft) tall.

Longest cave system
Recently it was found that two long cave systems in Kentucky, are actually connected to one another. These are the Mammoth Cave and the Flint Ridge cave systems. Together these consist of 530 km (330 miles) of underground passages and chambers.

▷ Using paints made from rock chemicals, plant juices and animal blood, people thousands of years ago painted these scenes on a cave wall. Many caves in Australia, North America, southern Europe and northern Africa have paintings such as these. Most of what we know about the everyday lives of ancient people comes from the cave paintings and the remains of primitive fires found in cave entrances.

Index

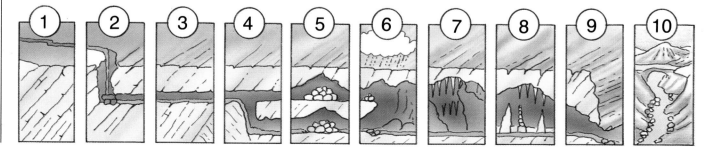

PRINTED IN BELGIUM BY
proost
INTERNATIONAL BOOK PRODUCTION